Numbers

Can you count from 1 to 5?

1 one

How many flowers can you see?

two

2

How many fish are swimming?

3

three

How many balls is the clown juggling?

four

4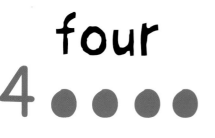

How many candles are on the cake?

five

5 ●●●●●

How many shells are there?

Shapes

Everything is made of shapes. Can you see any of these shapes in your home?

Rectangle Surprises

What shape is the book?

a rectangle

a circle

What shape is the dog's ball?

a star

What shape is the top
of the fairy's wand?

a square

What shape is the window?

What shape is
the sail?

a triangle

Opposites

The opposite of **happy** is **Sad**.
Here are some more opposites:

The bowl is **hard**.

The kitten's fur is **Soft**.

up

The see-saw moves **up** and **down**.

down

This horse is **big**.

This horse is **small**.

The rabbit is **in** the hat.

The rabbit is **out** of the hat.

This teddy bear's tie is **short**.

This teddy bear's tie is **long**.

First Words

Look around your home and try
to find some of these things.

brush

comb

mirror

bed

doll